YOU CAN DO IT!

Inspiration and motivation
for those daring to dream BIG

NOLAN W. MCCANTS

YOU CAN DO IT!
Copyright © 2012
Author: Nolan W. McCants

Nolan W. McCants
P. O. Box 9352
Naperville, IL 60567-9352
630-904-6262

www.nolanmccants.com
www.facebook.com/nolanmccants

ISBN: 0615566006
ISBN-13: 9780615566009

Printed in United States of America

Contents

Dedication

To my wife Gloria who has been a consistent voice of confidence and encouragement for nearly three decades. My best friend, you have been my number one cheerleader even while seeing me in both my weakest and strongest moments.

Acknowledgements

Far too many to name, thanks to the many voices and models that have provided inspiration, motivation and encouragement over the years. The journey thus far has been a blast and I cannot wait to see what the future will bring. Simon Presland and his editing skills, Angee Byrd, Monica Chambers and Michelle Williams for having those extra sets of much needed eyes, and Mrs. Stephanie Egler with the graphic tools were all very much of great value to me throughout this project.

I am most appreciative for the many wonderful people all over the world who are dear to me in so many ways. You all inspire me to live life to the fullest and are a testimony of my great wealth in global relationships. I am thankful for my family who create the atmosphere of joy that helps fuel my passions.

Foreword

If there were ever a book full of positive vibes it's this one. I've been greatly anticipating Nolan McCants' new work and he hasn't disappointed me. In my circle, McCants is known as "McCan." It strikes me as ironic that someone with such a gift for simplifying the complex, emboldening the timid, and making us all less cozy with can't. It's as if he was born to press us to decide daily which of these words we will choose and accept as our reality. And may I predict that once you've read this book you will want to refer to him as "McCan" as well.

I will take the prediction one step further and say that Nolan McCants *will* be one of those who is "referred" to, and this book will be heralded among his many accolades. Within these pages, McCants makes an airtight case to push ourselves beyond what we accept as our limits by providing solid and clear steps to accomplish—to make real—our dreams.

From my own "jazz" perspective, I immediately smiled as I read his inspiring words. I saw the connection between McCants' fearlessness and that of my improvisation as a jazz musician. *(It is easy to trace the genesis of this connection from Nolan's childhood; his father being a professional jazz musician.).* My music moves my audiences and McCants' words will stir you as well. They will awaken your inner determination; they will exhort you to greater heights, and motivate you to step up. Once you've been told, "Yes, you can do it!" it's hard to be satisfied with the word "No." This is the fuel that McCants pours into this book.

As an improviser, one lives an exhilarating life in a world of possibilities - the next note, the next phrase, the next idea, all depend on our courage to "step out into your destiny." Rather than plying us with mundane platitudes, Nolan provides solid evidence from his own multiple accomplishments and hurdles cleared. His successes are proof that he's lived out the words in this book, and he energizes our determination to fulfill our dreams.

Finally, as one who stepped out to learn how to speak French and Spanish (and a skosh of Japanese) I was quickly able to make the connection between McCants' wise advice regarding *fear of rejection* and moving past it. The person who is afraid to make a mistake will never learn. It is in fact through making mistakes that we all learn new ways of doing things, which can evolve into bigger and better dreams. As McCants dutifully teaches us, this is especially true when it comes to moving forward into the uncharted territory of dreams that become reality.

This is truly the stuff that life is made of!

Kirk Whalum
Saxophonist & CEO of the Stax Museum of American Soul Music & Stax Music Academy

You Can Do It!

Early in life I realized how blessed and fortunate I was to have an incredible home life. Although neither of my parents ever achieved fame or wealth—they never owned their own home, never traveled the world, and did not leave a financial inheritance for their children—they provided a deeply loving environment. They also demonstrated excellence in everything they did, no matter their place in life. These values are worth more to me than all the riches the world could offer.

My dad was a professional jazz musician, yet he was counted among those starving artists who were perhaps born before their time. Even though he had phenomenal talent, he was never able to translate his abilities into great monetary gains. Yet I watched my dad spend countless hours at home, sometimes in near darkness, practicing his craft so that he would always perform to his optimal ability. Why? My dad was extremely conscious about doing everything with a heart of excellence, even to the point of dressing impeccably for a walk to the corner store. *Excellence was in his bones.*

My mom also lived life and worked with a mindset of excellence. She spent years cleaning the homes of the wealthy, and I spent many summer days sitting in these mansions waiting for her to complete her tasks. They were literally the homes of the rich and famous. Yet I never sensed that my mother was simply domestic help; she worked with such distinction and quality and I felt proud to be her son. She would later become a nurse, and she was always valued and appreciated for the level of quality she brought with her.

My brother, Glenn, and I are now involved in vocations that require excellence in order to achieve success. I can't tell you how many times I've reflected on my childhood experiences and thanked God for the lessons my parents taught us.

There was something else that took place in my home, and truthfully I'm not even sure that my parents were aware of it. No matter what my brothers and I decided to pursue, whether a temporary project or some long-term pursuit, our parents never gave us the impression that we could not accomplish our goals; rather we were constantly encouraged that we could!

As a consequence, when I was young, I would move from idea to idea, and project to project, without any fear of the possibility of failure; I never thought that a task was beyond my ability. When I reflect back on having started a public relations firm at the tender age of eighteen, with no real education or experience in this area, it seems ridiculous. Yet my dream grew into reality and a successful one at that. (I contend that ignorance can be a blessing at times. It's only when we are convinced of what we cannot do that we do not try.)

I realize that we all come from different backgrounds. Some are born into poverty while others are born with a silver spoon in their mouths. But we all have the God-given ability to dream, to value, to create what ifs and possibilities; to explore, to visit every possibility before us that can combine into key ingredients for success. And we can do whatever is before us with excellence!

Our imagination is so very powerful. When I was a child, I was a thinker, a dreamer, one who imagined all kinds of possibilities; I visited places in my mind all the time. I was raised in the western suburbs of Chicago. From my suburban street on a clear day I could gaze at the peaks of the skyscrapers that line the city sky. They fascinated me. I would dream of the hustle and bustle, being present in its midst, and all of the things that must take place in that big city. I was also extremely inquisitive. There wasn't a business in my neighborhood that I did not visit, inviting myself in, meeting the owner, and asking questions about what he or she did. I knew every owner by name, and I had free reign to roam through their businesses, asking questions that only a child could, and I felt the liberty to do so. It unlocked something within me, a yearning to go and explore my world as I grew older. Thus, even at a young age, I began to collect information, insights, and wisdom. This has never changed. Even today, at nearly fifty years of age, I'm still inviting myself into places and I continue to dream.

As a dreamer I dream big, and I've discovered that dreams beget dreams. By following our passions we intersect with our destiny. As we pursue our dreams, there is a process of discovery that will take us into deeper and more expansive dreams. Some dreams will make it to fruition, while others will simply serve as stepping stones.

Dreams don't just happen; they don't just come to pass without our participation. There must be a strategy and a plan in place to pursue our dreams. Day by day, here a little there a little, dreams really do come to pass.

When passion fuels a dream, it is imperative to always give your best and to remain focused, never concerning yourself too much with the opinions of others as to whether or not your dream is viable. Simply set out to achieve success. Sometimes I succeed and sometimes I fall short. But what's most important is that I have dreamed, I have done my best with a spirit of excellence, that I have passion, and that I never stop trying.

At this point in my life I've experienced the realization of some major dreams: I have created and developed a full-service public relations firm, serving just about every industry under the sun; I'm approaching my sixteenth year as founding pastor of a thriving ministry;

I have authored several books; I'm called on to speak around the world; and most recently I have been recognized as an award-winning fine arts photographer. There are also many smaller dreams that have come to fruition along the way. I am doing what I love and have already superseded anything I ever thought I could achieve at this stage in my life or in life, period.

I've written this book to encourage you to pursue your dreams. What dreams do you have that spark passion and yearning within you? What do you envision doing but have not yet pursued? I encourage you to go for it! Dreams are birthed into success that began in the minds of some of the most ordinary, obscure people—people just like you and me. Dreams do not always depend on affluence, influence, adequate resources, the best education, having the right connections, or even being the most brilliant person. But they do depend on you exploring every possible avenue and doing all that is within your means.

Yes, you can succeed with your dreams; if I can, you can, too.

You can do it!

1

Dare to Dream

How many times have you viewed some extraordinary architecture, interacted with the latest technology, or utilized a unique service and wondered, *Wow, what genius thought of that?* It's really amazing when you ponder a new invention and realize how much creative work went into it. Every day we are touched by and experience the reality of someone else's dream.

The truth of the matter is that rarely is "genius" involved. In most cases, history shows that necessity was truly the mother of invention. Someone had a need and the process of pondering different options or ways of doing things produced thinking that brought about the solution. Often it wasn't an expert who had specialized training or education or previous experience. It was the average Joe or Jane who asked, "What if?" What we consider to be extraordinary was envisioned with out-of-the-box thinking and actions predicated on what was imagined. By banishing doubt and putting wheels in motion, the average person can enter the hallowed halls of "genius" along with those innovators who have become important contributors to this world. How incredible is that! The bottom line is, if you have a positive, I-won't-be-denied mindset and an ability to dream, then you can join the ranks of those who create, innovate, and invent.

Dreams start with an incredible gift called *imagination*. Imagination is something we often dismiss. It's that unique human ability to paint pictures in our minds of things that have never been seen before; or if it has already been invented, then imagination can be called upon to improve the invention. Dreaming is that extraordinary creative ability we all possess to envision things that are not, but with some nurturing and diligence can become reality. Dreaming is the ability to transpose onto a blank landscape the endless possibilities of your own thoughts; you envision how things could be if only given the opportunity.

Dreams are where thoughts exist without limitations, boundaries, or restrictions encountered in the physical world. No judgments, no critiques, and without precedence. Just possibility. The "What if?" factor is allowed to run freely and uninterrupted. Arriving unannounced, a dream comes sometimes subtly and sometimes with great fanfare. With or without prompting they abruptly manifest themselves, popping into our minds, producing the urge to do something different.

Dreaming is the ability to transpose onto a blank landscape the endless possibilities of your own thoughts; you envision how things could be if only given the opportunity.

A sad, but very unfortunate fact is that many dreams die in the mind of the dreamer; the individual was either unconvinced their dream had value or they lacked the confidence to believe their dream could actually come true. Many dreams are never shared or voiced aloud; they remained locked in the mind and heart of the conceptualizer. Yet there are countless people throughout the ages who have refused to succumb to disillusion.

Consider the following four people:

- We owe a great debt of gratitude to George Washington Carver, who's inventions and contributions include: using soybeans to make plastic; turning wood shavings into synthetic marble; converting cotton into paving blocks; crop-rotation methods giving special emphasis to the nitrogen replenishing role of legume products; and well over 300 peanut-products and sweet potato based products.

- Born into poverty and segregation in Kansas in 1912, Gordon Parks became one of the most influential men in America before his death in 2006. From his humble beginnings of employment in the Farm Security Administration (FSA), Parks became one of our nation's most famous and sought after photographers, including two decades at *Life Magazine*. His talents also led to writing—he wrote twenty books, including the *Sun Stalker* and *A Hunger Heart*—and Hollywood—he contributed to eleven movies, including *Shaft!* and *Super Cops*. He was truly a man who lived out his dreams, and his legacy lives on through the Gordon Parks Foundation.

- In 1965, Stephanie Kwolek invented one of the modern world's most readily recognized and widely used materials: Kevlar. Kevlar is the super strong, but lightweight synthetic material used in bulletproof vests. Her name appears on 16 patents and she is sole patent holder on seven.

- Under CEO Helen Greiner's leadership, iRobot Corporation has become a world leader in robotic technology, supplying robots for the industrial, consumer, academic, and military markets. You have probably seen or heard of the ROOMBA robotic vacuum that was introduced to the consumer products marketplace in 2002.

These men and women toiled in humble obscurity before their dreams propelled them onto the main stage of life. But for every person who has become "famous" there are countless men and women just like you and me who have lived out their dreams and impact our lives in so many ways.

Indeed, the world needs what your heart is dreaming about.

It's my personal dream to encourage you to dream and to dream frequently. But to stop there would be a disservice to you. I must challenge you to *pursue* those dreams, because the world awaits what is hidden in your heart. Indeed, the world *needs* what your heart is dreaming about.

Take action

As one who has dreamed and gone on to pursue his dreams to fruition, I have encountered many people with great imaginations, hopes, and desires over the years. When people with dreams connect with those who have followed their hearts, sparks are sent flying through the imagination, fueling these individuals with hope and an I-can-do-it-too attitude. If given the opportunity, people can literally spend hours and days just talking about their dreams. It's always exciting to see enthusiasm in their eyes and hear passion in their voices.

In order to separate the dreamers from the doers, I ask the hard questions about steps they've taken to make their dreams a reality. At this point, a clear divide is made between those who will experience the journey of their lives and those who will remain in dreamland, never awaking their creative experience. As a motivator, I always give a firm nudge in an attempt to rouse the latter from their slumber and push them toward their destiny.

Make it a reality

Throughout your life you may have countless dreams. But there is usually one dream that possesses you. It is so vivid that it engages all of your senses. You can literally feel it, smell it, hear it, taste it. It appears in your mind's eye when you're asleep; and in your waking hours it remains extraordinarily clear in the mental theater of your mind. It draws you in, challenging you, even daring you to take the next courageous step. I say to you, "Make this dream a reality!"

Because we are all uniquely wired and have differing personalities, we pursue things in our own ways and in our own time, so I am reluctant to be too specific in giving direction to bring your dream to fruition. However, there are some simple and practical steps you can take toward fulfillment. Taking these steps will create a comfort level for you; they will increase your self-confidence and help set you up for success:

- **Write your dreams down on paper.**
  Take time to revisit your thoughts often, reminding yourself of the limitless possibilities. Feel free to modify your dream, your goal, your purpose, as you move forward and discover greater potential. Let the words, "What if?" guide you and let your imagination flow.

- **Be selective about who you share your dreams with and don't expect a lot of encouragement.** Pioneering can be a lonely place. A word of caution: I've watched people make enemies of friends and family because the latter couldn't see the person's vision. Those who are close to you are not against you; they just don't understand and are more concerned about you than your dream that they have not yet seen.

- **It's a good idea to have a diverse balance of people around you.** There are those who will love you like a mama and would encourage you no matter what obstacles you face. Others will ask probing questions in an effort to help you succeed. They will challenge your theories and cause you to think about the very real nuts and bolts of making your dreams become reality. And don't disregard the naysayers. They can give you added resolve to accomplish your plans and prove them wrong. As you pursue your dream, you will cross paths with fellow dream chasers who have been there, weathered the storms that oppose creativity, and have made their dream a reality.

- **There will come a point in time where your dream and the reality of life's limits and restrictions intersect.** At this point you will need to do the math. What will it cost you in time, money, and resources? Write these down. At first this may seem overwhelming and even discouraging. But don't let obstacles stop you; they present an opportunity to grow your dream while growing you on a personal level. Don't become despondent with not being able to see how your dream will come together. Remember, dreamers dream; those who are willing to do the work bring their dream to fruition. Just keep chipping away. Don't be afraid to modify or reduce the scope of your dream in order to at least get in the game.

> There will come a point in time where your dream and the reality of life's limits and restrictions intersect. At this point you will need to do the math.

- **Be careful of becoming overly anxious.** Delay is a natural part of the process that also presents incredible opportunities for growth and discovery. Always remember that dreams beget dreams. Relax and enjoy the ride.

- **Focus and make specific time for dream development daily or at least weekly.** Yes, it's true that every little bit counts. Put one foot in front of another and keep moving forward. You will have some highly productive periods and times where everything seems to grind to a halt. Sometimes it's good to step away, get refreshed, and come back stronger.

Just know that you can do it!

Thoughts to Ponder

What did this chapter say to you?

What did this chapter prompt you to do?

Getting It Done Action Items

1. _____

2. _____

3. _____

4. _____

5. _____

Notes to Self

2

Power of Curiosity

Curiosity is key to discovery and enriched learning. It's essential to expanding your world and enlarging your creative capacity. Curiosity will broaden your view of life, people, opportunity, and your sense of adventure. It will give you a greater awareness of things that are around you. Through curiosity, you can solve the unknown; it can demystify and simplify the complex.

There's an old proverb that I'm sure you've heard: "Curiosity killed the cat." It is a warning against being too curious lest you be harmed in some way. The proverb was used as early as 1598, in which British playwright, Ben Jonson, used it in his play *Every Man in His Humour*. Now curiosity may have killed the cat, but we cannot ignore our natural sense of curiosity. Without curiosity, how would inventions become a reality? How would diseases be cured? How would anyone get ahead in life?

The curious person is someone who probes, looking beyond the surface and investigating to see what makes something tick. Either by deliberate action or by instinct, curiosity directs attention to obscure details and facts. Acted upon, curiosity asks questions, analyzes, then asks more questions. It rarely accepts the first answer as the only answer. Curiosity drives you to press in and press on; you seek to unveil the hidden and answer the unknown. Curiosity is the desire to have a

Curiosity is the desire to have a deeper knowledge into what causes things to be the way they are and how to improve upon them.

deeper knowledge into what causes things to be the way they are and how to improve upon them.

I just happen to be naturally inquisitive. I have always loved talking to people, those who are interesting and inspiring, and those who are solid everyday folk. I enjoy getting to know how people think and comprehend life. I also relish a challenge; I like to try to figure out how things work and how something can be done another way.

Deliberate curiosity

Now being curious for curiosity sake is okay. It's okay to ask a question, receive an answer, and move on. But I'm talking about being curious on *purpose*. For instance, in my public relations business, we focused on developing collateral materials—brochures, sales tools, promotional materials, that sort of thing. Because I owned the business, I became highly sensitized to anything graphic. It didn't matter whether it was a billboard, magazine, or a newspaper ad; my eyes would investigate every detail of anything visual, and I'd ask questions about the use of color schemes, shapes, photo techniques, and lines, while taking mental notes. I have ripped out pages of a magazine and taken them back to the "lab" to see how I could borrow a technique or two. My inquisitive side was extremely helpful in enlarging my graphic signature. I was able to create graphics with unique and varying looks, and avoided being trapped into reproducing the same mundane work. All that we do is a mosaic of what we take in, and curiosity is the catalyst we use to capture ideas, knowledge, and experience.

What are you curious about? What piques your interests? What have you done to feed your curiosities? I encourage you to let your curiosity lead you in life. Don't just rely on another person's discoveries. Yes, books, research, and clinical studies are fine. But there is nothing better than direct exposure. If you want to know more about bees, don't just read about them; seek out someone who raises them and get the information first hand. And don't stop with one person; go to another and another until your curiosity is satisfied.

> **Don't just rely on another person's discoveries. Yes, books, research, and clinical studies are fine. But there is nothing better than direct exposure.**

You Can Do It!

A curious path

I have discovered that everyone speaks and shares out of a personal, but limited journey. The path for one is always different than the path taken by another. One person may have taken a direct route to their destiny, while someone else stumbled into theirs. We can learn from both, but there may be greater insights gleaned from the latter. Whatever route these individuals took, curiosity was right there every step of the way, fueling their creative side, and spurring their imagination. I encourage you to be exhaustive in your being curious. Keep asking questions as long as they continue to surface. But don't just ask questions for the sake of questioning. Gather knowledge and let it further fuel your curiosity.

I love and am a strong advocate of international travel. Here in America we have been duped into believing that we have the better way of doing things. So much so, that we go to other countries and arrogantly attempt to impose our culture, instead of learning from those we encounter. I encourage you to travel to destinations that will spark your curiosity. Don't be shy and don't limit your travels. But go with an open mind to explore and learn. There are many diverse ways to get the same thing done. Curiosity will cause you to seek out different avenues, taking what's useful and discarding what is not, or perhaps shelving an idea for another time and place.

What questions do you have about the world around you? Don't just ask the question; allow your curiosity to lead you to answers. Curiosity can be your confidante on a wonderful journey of discovery and understanding. Nothing is ever lost when you collect a broad range of knowledge, interesting facts and figures, and obscure trivia. Who knows when you might come across the very thing that leads to your becoming who you were made to be?

Jot down a list of things that spark your curiosity. Consider things that you have never looked into and ask yourself, *Why not?* Curiosity can be the very thing you've been missing to truly start living. Put a simple plan in motion and follow through until you've satisfied the full extent of your curiosity.

In most cases, people who have dismissed their natural tendency to be curious have done so because of a sense of discomfort or fear: the feeling of not belonging; the thought of not being able to accomplish a goal or fulfill a dream; or the inability to transition into something new. If curiosity is going to catapult you into experiencing all that life has to offer, then it's imperative to address your fears or apprehensions. Only you can decide to do this. Only you can challenge them and overcome them by allowing curiosity to get the better of you. Go ahead; develop your inquisitive nature. Become more purposeful in your seeking to know.

Knock on the door

You might be surprised to discover that when you ask someone if a door is open, they will respond with a definitive, "No!" The sad reality is that most are answering out of their own assumptions; they've lost their sense of curiosity. They're uncertain about

I've always told my children, 'Don't let anyone tell you a door isn't open. Knock for yourself and if there's no answer, then turn the knob.'

themselves and about what is on the other side of the door. They've never tried the door for themselves, and they never will because they assume it will never open. It's a default "rejection complex" that many seem to possess. I guarantee that if you knock you will reap the rewards. You'll also find out there are many more open doors than suspected.

I've always told my children, "Don't let anyone tell you a door isn't open. Knock for yourself and if there's no answer, then turn the knob." Few people allow their curiosity to give them the initiative to follow through and persist when denied. You can never afford to take someone else's word for it.

In a later chapter, we will look at the value of "opportunity." The truth is that opportunity awaits the curious and the curious won't be denied. Many times you have to press your way into your destiny. What is in you will cause you to grow and explore. Things happen for people who make them happen, and good things happen to people who are curious. Taking a passive, uninvolved role will not lead to success.

Let your curiosity lead you to greater opportunities and greater success.

You can do it!

Thoughts to Ponder

What did this chapter say to you?

What did this chapter prompt you to do?

Getting It Done Action Items

1. _____

2. _____

3. _____

4. _____

5. _____

Notes to Self

3

The Fear Factor

When I was a boy, after awaking from a bad dream, I would have to talk to myself and convince myself it was only a dream. But oftentimes the dark would fuel my imagination and I would conjure up images of things in the shadows. I was afraid. If I couldn't convince myself of their unreality, I would make a mad dash into my parent's room. As an adult, if I awaken after a bad dream and am in a partial sleep state, I sometimes have to remind myself that the dream was not real. But I may still have a difficult time getting back to sleep.

We've all had disturbing dreams or frightening dreams. These types of dreams are often driven by fear. Yet this debilitating fear factor is not limited to the nighttime; many people, who would otherwise be very successful in life, have allowed fear of one type or another to keep them from moving forward. When listening to people, I am amazed how many of them convincingly talk themselves out of pursuing their dreams because of what they fear. It is not their personal experience that bears out their fears. In most cases, it's their own fearful imagination that stops them dead in their tracks.

Fear is a belief. It is an emotional reaction caused by the perception that someone or something is a threat, perhaps dangerous, or likely to cause pain. Yes, there are real fears. They can come in the form of a health issue, or because of an oncoming car after you step into the street. However, when it comes to us fulfilling our personal dreams, fear of the unknown and the "what if?" can quickly paralyze us.

Understanding fear

While browsing the Internet, I came across a site that listed names of fears and phobias.

Curiosity got the best of me and I started counting the names listed. However, I stopped counting at well over 300, but I was only halfway through the list!

At a conference I once heard the best definition of the word "fear." The speakers used the acronym, F.E.A.R, and said that it stood for "False Evidence Appearing Real." I've also heard that up to 90 percent of the things we fear never become a reality; they are only real in our minds.

Whether real or imagined, fear causes a fight or flight response within us; we either become angry and stand our ground, or we run from that which we fear. In a life threatening situation we might run, but if someone threatens our spouse or children, we will stay and stand up for them. At work,

Will we choose to double our determination to fulfill our dreams or will we allow fear to lead us into the grip of sorrow and regret?

we might fear missing a project deadline, so we stay and double our efforts to finish on time. We also might fear standing up in front of coworkers to give a presentation, so we call in sick on the day of our discourse. In relation to dreams, fear also causes a fight or flight response. We must ask ourselves, Will we choose to double our determination to fulfill our dreams or will we allow fear to lead us into the grip of sorrow and regret?

Fear and self-talk

Here is a psychological principle that I want you to understand: thoughts dictate emotions, and emotions dictate actions and reactions. Fear is often referred to as an emotion, but the truth is it is a thought first. Where do fearful thoughts and mindsets come from? Our self-talk. Now stay with me as I explain what self-talk is, and you'll see how it can create fears that control us.

During every waking moment of our lives, we are in a constant dialogue with ourselves. Our inner minds speak to us and interpret what we are seeing and hearing according to predetermined filters or mindsets we have that were formed through our experiences in life. It is said that we "speak to ourselves" up to 300 words a minute, but speak to others only 140 words a minute. Our internal voice determines how we perceive a situation, whether negative or positive. Our self-talk includes our conscious thoughts as well as our unconscious beliefs. Our beliefs are what we see as "truth" based on our experiences.

Much of our conscious self-talk can be reasonable (e.g. "I'd better finish my report for my boss." or "I'm really looking forward to the weekend."). However, much of our subconscious self-talk can be negative, unrealistic, and self-defeating (e.g. "I'm a failure. Everyone hates me. I'm hopeless."). Our subconscious self-talk is what really controls our emotions and plays itself out in our actions and reactions. Thus, a fearful subconscious mindset is the root of the fears we feel. Now that may sound obvious, but how many of us really stop to *listen* to what we are saying to ourselves? Rarely do we do this; instead, we allow our emotions to dictate what we are going to do, what we will say, and how we will react.

When it comes to understanding how fear affects us—or any emotion for that matter—we need to slow down or quiet our minds. We must discipline ourselves to hear what we are really saying to ourselves. We must hear negative messages we are speaking to ourselves that project fear into our present situation. Then we must ask ourselves, *Is what I am saying to myself really true?* If it is not true, then we must find out where our negative self-talk originated.

For instance, if my self-talk is, "I'm a loser; I'm a failure" then I will never succeed in fulfilling my dreams. In fact I will never even consider venturing out. I must then be willing to do some digging into my past. As a child, did my parents tell me that I was an idiot; that I'd never amount to anything? Did school bullies corner me on the playground and tease me or beat me up? Did I answer a question in class and get laughed at because my answer was wrong? These are just a few of our experiences that can cause us to develop negative self-talk about ourselves because it has rooted itself as "truth" in our minds.

Fear of failure

I believe that fear of failure is the root cause of most dreams dying in the recesses of a person's mind. It is perhaps the strongest force holding people

In a world full of uncertainty, fear of failure causes most people to "play it safe."

back from fulfilling their dreams. In a world full of uncertainty, fear of failure causes most people to "play it safe." Yet those who really desire to move forward choose to face this fear head on.

In order to overcome the fear of failure, the first thing we must do is to redefine the way we view failure—the belief we have about it. Our mindset will determine whether we go into "fight" or "flight" mode. The truth is that failure is a *critical element* in the science of achieving success. (Note: Webster's describes science as the "knowledge or a system of knowledge covering general truths, or the operation of general laws especially as obtained and tested through scientific method.") Failure is not a negative—as most people see it—but a positive motivator in life. Failures are really stepping stones toward the science of gaining the knowledge and truth we need to succeed. We cannot avoid failure; it is part of the natural order, and we simply cannot

Yet those who really desire to move forward choose to face this fear head on.

"achieve" or "win" at everything we set our minds to. However, through experience and learning, failure can be greatly minimized. Failure is neither the final score nor the end of our dreams. In fact, it's just the beginning of the journey toward success. Failures become guide posts, landmarks, and critical reminders of what not to do again.

> **Failure is neither the final score nor the end of our dreams. In fact, it's just the beginning of the journey toward success. Failures become guide posts, landmarks, and critical reminders of what not to do again.**

The second thing we must do is embrace failure. Yes, that's right, embrace it! No one has ever encountered failure without taking steps to achieve something— something that is bigger than themselves. Our revered former president, Abraham Lincoln, is a great example of one who overcame multiple failures.[1] Failure is the gateway to gaining wisdom, humility, knowledge, understanding, and respect for established truths and laws. The way we navigate our failures will determine how well we handle our successes. My advice: don't give in to whatever fuels your fear of failure. Instead face it. Examine it. Decide that whatever you believe to be true about failure is only an obstacle to overcome and not the final word. Question your fear and find out why it has a debilitating power in your life. Remember, you have the power to overcome that which is trying to stifle your dreams and hinder your forward progress.

Fear of the unknown

Most people fear what they don't know, and ignorance can either be a curse or a blessing. I often reflect on starting my first business. Not yet twenty years of age, and having no formal education or prior experience in the industry, I was fearless and naive enough to believe that I could use my natural gifts and talents to succeed in my venture of creating and running a public relations firm. Had I been consciously aware of, or more "educated" about what it took to establish a successful business, I may never have begun the journey.

Instead of fearing the unknown, I challenged it! I converted the unknown from enemy to ally. As the business grew, I was able to realize levels of success that I had always dreamed possible. Now, I'm not suggesting that everyone should start a business from a position of ignorance. However, I am strongly suggesting that you not allow any perceived obstacle hinder you from pursuing your dreams. For instance, you might have an idea to develop a product that you feel will revolutionize an industry. Or you might want to start a small business based on an existing product, but one that you have a unique way of marketing. One of the first sets of questions you will ask yourself is, *Do I really have something of value? Will anyone buy my product? Is it really worth what I think it's worth?* These questions cannot be answered until you are willing to step out of your comfort zone, beyond fear.

Remember, when pioneering there may not be sufficient data to prove whether or not something is possible. You must, therefore, move forward using trial and error. Through this process you will develop a knowledge base that can never be taken away from you. You will also experience first hand certain laws that either allow or prevent movement in certain directions. Along the way you will have redefined your fear of the unknown by collecting a wealth of invaluable experiences. You can then capitalize on those experiences, establishing self-confidence, and emerging with a powerful knowing that replaces your fear of the unknown. Know that if you have ever failed at anything, then you're in good company. No one has ever achieved any measure of success without that essential ingredient called failure.

Fear of rejection

People who follow their dreams are a strange breed. They do not allow fear of rejection to hinder their set path. It's almost as though they are in a fog; they simply refuse to give in to the voice of rejection, whether that voice is in their own heads or uttered by those around them.

If you're going to be afraid of what people think, then you're doomed to fail right from the start. The fear of rejection is insurmountable for many people. The thought of what others think of my dream or what others might think if I fail is the root of shame, guilt, embarrassment and a whole lot of other hindering emotions. But those who succeed have already determined something: they won't let fear of being laughed at, or worse, being ridiculed, stop them from following their dreams. I'll let you in on a secret: those who criticize others or scorn another's dream, are jealous of anyone who wants to rise above. So what if you don't succeed? At least you have lived a little and you are a better person for it.

You must realize that the vast majority of people you will encounter during your dream-filled journey are filled with their own sense of rejection. They are reluctant to try anything because of what others might think and/or say and they have internalized this into perpetual self-rejection. They would rather play it safe than be sorry. It is true; misery loves company and they want you in their company.

Another reason why people frown upon risk takers is because the success of one who has stepped out may prove that playing it safe isn't the best route after all. Human beings can be very interesting creatures! Generally, society does not congratulate those who walk outside the lines and go their own way. This is why people who stay between the lines feel some measure of safety and security. There is comfort in believing that safety equals success, and this type of success is encouraged and applauded by the mainstream. Sadly, the masses are fed this message over and over again.

The fact is history shows that conformers are rarely recognized or recalled. It is those who dared to be different, who not only walked outside the lines but reset the boundaries who are both recognized and celebrated in life. So don't take the scrutiny and disdain of others as a personal affront; just remain diligent and focused on your dreams. You must develop thick skin and become disciplined at turning a deaf ear toward naysayers, doubters, and fear mongers. Remind yourself that most of them are operating out of a deficit position—their own fears—that you have already overcome. Keep in mind that your doubters today may very well become your students tomorrow.

It is those who dared to be different, who not only walked outside the lines but reset the boundaries who are both recognized and celebrated in life.

Stay positive. You can do it!

1. For an overview of Abraham Lincoln's life, go to http://www.historyplace.com/lincoln/

Thoughts to Ponder

What did this chapter say to you?

What did this chapter prompt you to do?

Getting It Done Action Items

1. _____

2. _____

3. _____

4. _____

5. _____

Notes to Self

4

Self-Education

No matter your pursuits or how much "formal education" you possess or pursue, there is nothing more enriching than self-education; it will teach you what no school can. It's what you do for you, to satisfy and advance yourself. It's the organic method of learning, and in my opinion the most fulfilling of all forms of education.

With self-education, each course of study is tailored to the student's interest. Classes are global and information is immediately applicable. It's done at your own pace, and the curriculum is based on your own natural inclinations and curiosities. You won't need the signatures of any academic gurus on a piece of paper to signify your acceptance into their world of higher education. The proof of what you learn through your own experience and understanding will certainly be found in the results. That is why it's called self-education.

Our planet is vast and it begs to be explored. Yet, most people are comfy in their own little safe and familiar worlds. Exposure is critical as it expands us and enlarges our desire to know and to understand. The more you take in, the more you'll want to take in. This is the essence of self-education.

On every level of life there are things that you can do to broaden your knowledge. A good place to start is by stepping out of your safety zones and diving into the unfamiliar worlds of various music genres, cuisines, cultures, generations, fashion, and geography. Pick a place on the map that you've never really thought about and go discover something new. Find some exotic cuisine that you've shied away from and chow down at the first available eatery. With each new discovery a new you will come to life and your zest for learning will explode.

Stay inquisitive

Let your inquisitive mind lead you on a quest for self-education by taking charge and digging into a subject. Most people love talking about the things they are passionate about, so don't be afraid to go directly to the source. For instance, I have picked up the phone to call an author of a book or the producer of a radio show and was connected directly to that individual.

When I have an interest in something I remain inquisitive and take notes. I try to repeat what I've heard so the person knows I am serious and that I am paying full attention. From my notes, I develop a personal checklist so that I can go back and pursue things of interest with greater vigor, or follow-up on some action to increase my level of self-education. If I have the opportunity, I will report back to the source on what I did with the information shared. Then the next conversation will yield an even greater depth of revelation.

Observation

Much can be learned from simple observation. Just to be present to watch, sense, gather can give you incredible insight. Many people totally miss this one. For instance, my wife, Gloria, spent quite a few years working in early childhood development. She is a big proponent of play and creating an atmosphere where children have the opportunity to observe and experience their environment. Yes the kids learned a lot, but so did Gloria as she observed each child's interaction. As adults we often ignore observation as we move with swiftness from place to place without giving notice to the things we pass. But being intentional in observing life around us lends itself to an incredible learning experience.

When in a room, I observe colors, shapes, the placement of objects, flaws in construction, lighting, textures, traffic flows. My senses

But being intentional in observing life around us lends itself to an incredible learning experience.

are always wide open to take all of this in. I then ask the questions of why a thing is the way it is. This exercise is one that I employ with most everything I encounter, and I am always observing to see and to know. I am training my mind to resist passivity and to be aggressive toward learning. Rarely does something get past me. I consider myself a student of life and I study hard. Thus, I get to know a little bit about everything, which is extremely useful when engaging people in conversation. Those I connect with bring with them a vast range of experiences. Whenever there is commonalty there is potential for relationship on many levels. And relationships matter!

Active listening

It's extremely important to be an active listener. Active listening involves hearing what is said, observing body language, and repeating or paraphrasing what was spoken in order to make sure you have heard correctly. Whenever I encounter someone I go into memory mode, first listening for and memorizing a person's name. (People love it when you remember them and then call them by name. I'm about seventy percent accurate at getting names right, and I'm working to do better.) Next, I focus in on what is being said. I have to dismiss any preconceptions or assumptions if I truly want to know something I may never have heard before, or even to reinforce some foreknowledge. The bottom line is that I have to be disciplined at taking in information and making the most out of the moments that may never occur again.

Travel

Travel is something that I really enjoy and has to rate at the top of my list of self-education experiences. I have already touched five continents with the goal to hit them all before I call it a day. When I travel, I refuse to be content with seeing the contrived tourist areas. I must touch the local culture. Traveling overseas costs a fraction of one college semester, and can deliver more than a four-year degree.

Before my daughters went to college, my wife and I were determined to expose them to as much of the world as possible. They have visited much of America, several European countries, and the African continent. I am hopeful they have now acquired my wanderlust and will go on to expand their travel list, thus expanding their self-education.

To experience culture first hand is the true definition of self-education. Doing so will dispel myths, arrest prejudices, calm fears, and multiply your appreciation for the extensive and incredibly interesting global community of which we are all a part. So much can be learned and unlearned when we travel. Priorities can be reorganized and emphasis placed on that which really matters in life. Overall, it is a wonderful experience to be immersed into world cultures.

Employment

When it comes to educating yourself, it can never be done completely from the outside. So when you want to know, go inside. But go in with a determination to know, not just to do. Many people, particularly those in the corporate world, go into the workplace with blinders on. They suffer with tunnel vision, only seeing what's before them—their assigned task or duty. When you want to know about a particular industry, get inside and soak it up. Now, this doesn't mean you have to be an executive to gain invaluable insights, but you have to avoid minimizing small opportunities.

There is a lot of information to be gleaned from the receptionist's desk or in the mailroom. I'm not suggesting doing anything unsavory. It's just a matter of having your eyes and ears open, asking pertinent questions, and engaging the right people. You must know your mission and discipline yourself to get it done. Learn, learn, learn!

For example, my first opportunity in commercial radio was crowd control at a job fair for the radio station. Yes, I was paid to stand and count heads as people entered in order to control the number of people coming in. Having done so with seriousness and excellence led to my being offered a paid internship with one the Chicago's top stations. That position led to other significant doors being opened and relationships established that have benefitted me for many years.

Forget the hype

There seems to be mystery and hype surrounding every industry. And, if you listen to those who pass themselves off as being "in the know," you will buy further into these bizarre quantities. I say, when you want to know go to the source. Dig deep and read anything you can get your hands on relating to a subject. With the advent of the Internet there is absolutely no excuse for not knowing. But get to the core of understanding the things that you are pursuing by ignoring the shroud of mystery and hyperbole.

Instead of the spectacular, look for the practical essentials that really make something work.

Instead of the spectacular, look for the practical essentials that really make something work. Behind anything of worth will be principles, values, and methodologies that are consistent. It's best to hang your hat on these. Go for it.

You can do it!

Thoughts to Ponder

What did this chapter say to you?

What did this chapter prompt you to do?

Getting It Done Action Items

1. _____

2. _____

3. _____

4. _____

5. _____

Notes to Self

5

Managing Opportunity

Oh, the ever elusive opportunity. It comes and goes, sometimes without us giving it a second thought. Some opportunities are created, while others just show up in the most unusual circumstances. Some appear once, then vanish forever, while others visit us continually as we grow and develop, offering yet another invitation.

Problems and opportunities

If you have the correct mindset, then you can see opportunity in every problem. The word "problem" comes from the Latin *problema*, meaning something thrown forward.

Those who turn problems into opportunities have a knack of avoiding being at the *effect* of what's going on around them by consistently embracing difficult challenges to gain positive results.

Opportunity can be defined as "the circumstances that arise, making it possible to advance or increase." It's been my experience that opportunity always intersects with a prepared and ready mindset. It's also been my experience that, sadly, too many opportunities are

Some opportunities are created, while others just show up in the most unusual circumstances. Some appear once, then vanish forever, while others visit us continually as we grow and develop, offering yet another invitation.

wasted or ignored by those who cannot recognize what is in front of them.

During my high school career, I observed something that will remain with me for the rest of my life. My school, Proviso East, in west suburban Chicago, was and is a basketball powerhouse, churning out basketball standouts year after year. One such star was Glenn "Doc" Rivers with whom I shared the same graduating class. Glenn certainly stood out, breaking school records and setting others that still stand.

There was another very promising athlete on the same team as Glenn. In fact, many felt that this young man had equal, if not better, skills than Glenn did. But when opportunity presented itself, this young man was unable to seize the moment because of some character issues. No one had taught him that opportunities can be fleeting and he must be ready for action at all times. The same opportunity was presented to both young men. One man faded into obscurity, while Glenn went on to the NBA, becoming a star player and a winning coach.

Two important keys

The keys to opportunity are expectancy and preparedness. You must be armed with the understanding that opportunities show up on their own timetable. It's never a matter of if, but when. They might loom around the corner or hover above our heads, ready to knock on the door of our consciousness when they feel the time is right. Sometimes loudly, but most often very quietly. We have to train ourselves to listen for and recognize when opportunity knocks, and be ready to open the doors of our minds at a moment's notice. We must also be careful not to measure opportunity by size or quantity. Big things sometimes do come in small packages, and life can be created or captured in a single moment. I caution you to be careful about the opportunities what you choose to reject or minimize.

We have to train ourselves to listen for and recognize when opportunity knocks, and be ready to open the doors of our minds at a moment's notice.

I'm not sure when, where, or how I developed the ability to see an opportunity coming. But I can smell it like the scent of an impending rainfall. I feel as though I have cheated when it comes to opportunity, as I've had more than my fair share of them.

And yet, when I see the opportunities afforded others, I sometimes feel cheated.

We need to understand that opportunity can disguise itself in negative and positive ways, and we must be discerning before we jump into the unknown. For instance, when I was about fourteen, my dad was dying of cancer. It wasn't a good time for our family. We lived in a huge apartment complex with a blend of people and a mix of opportunities. You might appreciate that some were good and others were not so good. With our family situation, I could have taken any of these and dramatically altered my destiny. Such was the case when I chanced upon an opportunity with a friend with whom I shared a love for music.

He asked that I accompany him into the city one day. There was a new program being offered to youth at the University of Illinois' Chicago campus called "New Identity Youth Media Workshop." Get this: it was the dream of a very unique and special dreamer, NJorog Tho-Biaz. Despite inadequate funding, he assembled a team of professionals to launch a program that would reach out to at-risk young people through hands-on radio broadcast training, to help kids get on the right track. I could smell this opportunity a mile away! He, however, only attended the camp a few times before going his own way. (Thirty years later, NJorog continues to dream and touch many lives in wonderful ways. He has become one of my closest and dearest friends.)

I have often asked myself whether it was his role in that moment to simply walk me toward an opportunity that would lead me to one avenue of my life's destiny. I became actively involved in NJorog's program, leading me to work in commercial broadcasting as a teen, and producing and hosting my own nationally syndicated show for a brief stint. This work prepared me for other fascinating opportunities. Now remember, opportunity showed up dressed as an invitation to walk with someone who was contemplating their own journey. My point is that we must keep our eyes open and our ears attentive to opportunity's knock.

An expectant heart

Many people never expect opportunity to come and as a consequence it bypasses them over and over. I encourage you to have a heart of expectancy for your next opportunity. But remember, it may not look the way you would imagine. Just be open—l-i-s-t-e-n; watch and be ready to walk through uncommon doors. Don't be like the crowd around you. There are too many people fixated on remaining within their comfort zones and they can't see what is coming around the corner. Expand your world. Meet new people. Visit places that have not interested you before—or maybe they have interested you, but you've never taken the time to venture out. Help opportunity to find you by removing the obstacles that limit or hinder your exposure. Your world may be too small, and it's up to you to expand it through expectancy; no one, and I mean no one, will do it for you, including the opportunity itself.

Be prepared

I often hearken back to the Boy Scout motto, "Be Prepared!" Preparedness is the substance that fuels opportunity. There is nothing more exhilarating than sensing the presence of opportunity and knowing, yes *knowing*, that you are ready for it. No fear, no reservation; your heart beats with anticipation as your mind screams, "Bring it on!"

As with opportunity, preparedness comes in different sizes and shapes. Allow me to introduce an idea to you. Preparedness comes when you have considered all the potential possibilities of a given opportunity, and you have full knowledge of each one. Yes, people do this every day and it's impressive! They follow a very strategic path that includes the best education that money can buy. They intern to gain experience and pad their resume. They meet with great success this way and lead incredibly fulfilled lives. This is indeed a valid way to prepare for opportunity.

However, there is also that serendipitous set of events that may introduce itself for which there is no specific preparedness, other than knowing that opportunity has presented itself. For instance, I recall in high school an average soccer player who parlayed his talents into becoming a tremendous field goal kicker for our football team, simply because the football coach asked him to try out. I know of many very successful people who, without experience or training, have walked through the door of opportunity because they were prepared to do so and now live successful and fulfilled lives. Opportunities came when these individuals did not even have an inclination of what they wanted to do in life. Nevertheless, their hearts were prepared, should events come their way. If stories were told the similarities would be consistent from person to person. These individuals had no idea they possessed a particular skill or ability until they were placed in situations to utilize their gifts and talents. When given the opportunity, their passion arose and soon surpassed everything in their lives.

I've known doctors who walked away from practicing medicine to become musicians. I witnessed lawyers who quit practicing law to become inner city youth leaders. And I watched a guy go from stacking bricks on construction sites to becoming one of Chicago's leading radio station dj's. All because of preparedness.

Preparedness and expectancy say, "I am not limited to who I thought I was or who others say I am. In fact I may be many things and have yet to discover them!"

Whether prepared through planning or prepared in their conscious minds, these people seized the opportunity presented to them. Preparedness and expectancy say, "I am not limited to who I thought I was or who others say I am. In fact I may be many things and have yet to discover them!"

Expect opportunity to show up in strange places. Be prepared to see it dressed in uncommon ways. Always open the door with a bright smile and warm greeting.

You can do it!

Thoughts to Ponder

What did this chapter say to you?

What did this chapter prompt you to do?

Getting It Done Action Items

1. _____

2. _____

3. _____

4. _____

5. _____

Notes to Self

6

Building Relationships

In order to get things done in the world you need other people and you need to develop lasting relationships. People are brought together through many things such as common interests, mutual relationships, work, and play. No matter where you are in life or what you're doing, it doesn't take long to discover that you need people and people need you. The truth is that if you lack the desire to establish and nurture relationships, your path to success will be severely hampered. Remember, strong relationships are solid capital that has an exchange rate higher than any currency on the planet.

Hopefully, you were taught the wisdom of not burning bridges at a young age. It's even more important to understand the value of intentionally building and maintaining mutually beneficial relationships. Those who cultivate this attribute will possess a significant edge over others. So let's discuss a few things that are invaluable when building relationships.

Everybody is somebody

Never minimize a relationship no matter how insignificant it may seem to be at the time. You never know who is connected to whom or who someone might become. You also never know where the simplest relationship might lead, so treat everybody like they're somebody and you will never go wrong. In fact, I recommend keeping the golden rule for relationships in the forefront of your mind: Do unto others what you would have them to do to you. Besides, being nice doesn't cost you anything and can profit you much.

Pride and arrogance have caused countless people to miss out on incredible opportunities because they failed to appreciate the power of cultivating relationships. I exhort you: don't be someone who looks down on others.

When I walk into restaurants that I frequent, I get great service on every level because I *genuinely* try to connect with everyone from the owner to the busboy. One time my wife and her friends went to a popular downtown Chicago restaurant that I have frequented. She had never been there without me. When she drove up, the valet welcomed her by name. (He remembered the car and the fact that I didn't just hand off my keys, not even acknowledging his presence like many would do. I knew his name, I looked him in the eye, and I don't doubt that I knew his children's names and ages. Of course I tipped well.) Gloria came home excited that even the valet knew who she was. Score!!! I have the same relationship with restaurant hosts. I can normally get an immediate seating on a Friday at dinner time without a reservation, while others wait for an hour if not two. Consistently treating all people with dignity and respect is always a win-win.

When in public relations, I represented a national mega-retailer who had expanded into the Chicago market. They wanted to make a connection with the Oprah Winfrey Show. Now I've never met Oprah, but I developed a relationship with a woman on her staff who always took my calls. One call and in a matter of moments I made the connection. Days later my clients were on the front row of the Oprah Winfrey Show. I came away with a win because of the significance of relationship capital.

I'm not at all suggesting that everyone you see should be viewed as the next possible connection. I've encountered that attitude and it's a real turnoff. It's like people who get on social networks purely for selfish reasons like selling their wares. You can sense it a mile away. So don't approach new relationships with an agenda written on your forehead. Savor the moment and just enjoy connecting with another interesting person. Take time to legitimately become interested in them and their lives. There is richness in knowing the journey and dreams of others whose paths you've been fortunate enough to cross. You never know; in the future you may be of mutual benefit and that would be great!

Bring something to the table

In any relationship you should expect there to be an exchange, a quid pro quo. You bring something and you receive something. As my real estate investor friend, Dora White-Merritt, would often say on the subject of business networking, "Nolan we are all going to be used, we just have to determine how much." Know what you possess, what you bring to the table, and be prepared to dole it out when the time comes. There will be times that you will be called upon and other times that you offer yourself. In any case, whatever you do, do it well, giving it your all, even when not being directly compensated. That attitude and act will deliver healthy relationship dividends for many years to come.

Think long-term

So many people operate in the moment, never considering the long haul. If you are hasty to get a return on a relational investment, you're not an investor

It is the consistency of your genuineness that will determine your value to others.

at all, you're a gambler. Relationships may take years to establish. It is the consistency of your genuineness that will determine your value to others. Likewise, in order to really know who you may be dealing with, it takes time to get to know who they truly are and what they are about. So, be patient—especially with those who turn you off at first—and allow the relationship to grow and mature. The good ones will last and yield a great harvest.

The value of a name

In relationship building there is nothing that stands stronger than a good name. Having a good name is the same as having a good reputation. And having a good reputation depends upon having good character. A good name will always make you a lightning rod for new relationships. Of course the opposite is true as well. A bad name travels even faster and will serve to repel others. The greatest values you can possess are credibility, integrity, and selflessness.

The greatest values you can possess are credibility, integrity, and selflessness.

People want to plug into solid people who are known for their uprightness *and* who can make things happen. Everybody wants to relate to someone who is trustworthy, dependable, and thought highly of. A good name goes a very long way no matter what line of business you're in. So endeavor to build and protect your good reputation; it is your most prized personal asset.

Don't squander your relationship capital

Wisdom says that there is a time to call in favors. However, just because you have certain contacts doesn't mean you have to use them. The less frequently you withdraw from your relationship bank, the more likely you are to get a desired response when you need it.

Save up your favors and let your account grow, allowing it to earn interest by continuing to grow your relationships. For instance, I would

The less frequently you withdraw from your relationship bank, the more likely you are to get a desired response when you need it.

much rather return more calls than I've made, keeping my account full. I like to save the major connections for major deals. I also need to maintain viable relationships. I cannot simply call on someone I've known for years for something I may need, having rarely connected with that person.

Know when and when not to tap into relationships. One too many knocks on any door can quickly demote you from being a friend to being called a mooch and a pest. The basic rule is to call in a favor only when you absolutely need to. And, ideally, don't call if you haven't made a recent or steady deposits into the relationship bank. How do you know if you're about to call on someone you really shouldn't? Listen to your gut-check. If you don't feel right, if you get a sense there's something wrong in calling, then don't do it! Make deposits by staying in touch, dropping an occasional note, sending an invitation to a function that could benefit the other person, drop off a small gift, enjoy a periodic meal together that you pay for, or send some business their way. All of these things matter when we talk about growing and developing relationships in the proper way.

Seek more to be a resource than use other people for what you can get. It's amazing what happens when you offer yourself to be available to help another's dreams come true. Be a source of encouragement, offer wisdom and advice, or become a bank of resources that others can use. You will never go wrong when you develop, grow, or maintain relationships in which you are seen in a positive light.

You can do it!

Thoughts to Ponder

What did this chapter say to you?

What did this chapter prompt you to do?

Getting It Done Action Items

1. _____

2. _____

3. _____

4. _____

5. _____

Notes to Self

7

Stay Focused

Whatever your dreams, pursuits, or aspirations, you must stay focused if you want to succeed. Once you are clear on your direction you'll want to put your all into seeing your dream through to the finish. However, when you're in the moment, when you're envisioning your dream fully displayed in your mind, elation will overtake you, and you cannot see any obstacles. But, when reality sets in as you begin your journey, it's easy to get distracted or side-tracked by the day-to-day. You also have to resist the temptation to chase after rabbits.

Rabbits are other ambitions, goals, and ideas you may have that compete with your original dream. Time spent hunting every rabbit and going down every rabbit trail can take away time, energy, and resources from your primary dream.

To stay on course and maintain your focus, I encourage you to create an idea folder where ideas and thoughts for future projects or ventures are deposited. You will find that some will remain valid and you'll want to follow up on them at a later time, while others may never make it out of the folder. Staying the course is a discipline that many struggle with, particularly those having creative minds. But it's necessary if you want to achieve success. Here's a tip: if you know that you aren't the disciplined type, then make sure you have those around you

If you know that you aren't the disciplined type, then make sure you have those around you who are, or your dream may simply remain in your mind.

who are, or your dream may simply remain in your mind.

Concrete steps

Staying on track begins by committing your plans to paper. Even if the direction changes, you should always have your thoughts spelled out along with how you will get things done. Then you won't be dismayed by the curve balls that come your way and you can work around them or even incorporate them into your plans. Be specific about the end goal and be realistic about what it will take to get there. And always remember that dreams take time, so be patient with yourself and your dream.

Written goals are key to maintaining focus and tracking progress. They provide measurement and enable you to determine the effectiveness of your efforts. They will also tell you whether you have been advancing forward or just treading water.

Many people disdain the front end planning process, but be assured; planning goals and direction will make accomplishing your dream a whole lot easier. Think of it in these terms:

Who gets into a car and starts down the road without a sense of where they're going and clear directions to help them reach their destination? This person takes twice as long to reach their destination. Don't let laziness or discomfort be the cause of needless delays. Take the time and plan your steps.

Written plans will help you avoid becoming overwhelmed by attempting to do too much too soon. They will help you to pace yourself; they will remind you dreams become reality one step at a time. Haste truly does make waste. A written plan will cause you to slow down and think things through so you can minimize needless mistakes. Concentrate on completing each step in an efficient and thorough manner, and your dream will become a reality in due time.

Along with your written plan, it's always a good idea to create timelines for yourself. Make a list of tasks along with targeted dates for completion. Be as detailed as you possibly can. Of course you'll need to modify and make changes as you move ahead in the process and that's to be expected. But written plans and goal setting will keep you on track and keep you moving forward.

Set achievable goals

Many people make the mistake of setting lofty, unattainable goals. That only serves to cause frustration and a feeling of defeat when goals aren't met. And, if you're working with others, this can negatively impact the morale of your team and call into question your ability to lead. So set goals that can be fully realized. Start with small steps, set bite sized achievements that create a, "Wow, we can do this!" mindset. Each accomplished goal will point the way toward whatever ultimate goal you have in mind. Make sure

Start with small steps, set bite sized achievements that create a, "Wow, we can do this!" mindset.

you factor in celebrations for milestones along the way. Find a special time and way to step back, savor your progress, and pat yourself on the back. It's good to say, "Hey I did it!" Your feelings of euphoria will stay with you for many days, and you deserve whatever accolades and rewards come your way.

Consider you!

This means paying attention to how you do things, what works and what doesn't, when touched by your hands. You'll need to be honest with yourself and own both your strengths and weaknesses. Many struggle with defining these because it's easy to be consumed by strength and overwhelmed by weakness. These are personal. A common problem is to make the mistake of comparing your weaknesses to another's strengths. But I caution you: don't become consumed by your strengths or weaknesses. Keep a balanced approach to both. Stay level headed, and you'll see your dream become a reality.

Teamwork

Nobody has it all. I am reminded of the early days of Michael Jordan's career. Alone with all the talent he possessed, it wasn't until other key players and a great coach were added that he realized the ultimate success on the court.

You need others to succeed. Period! If you remain a lone ranger, you may accomplish what you set out to do, but you'll also limit the size and scope of your dream. Your team can help in a number of areas: some members will keep you on track; others may warn you of potential pitfalls and help find ways around them; still others will be confidantes, people with whom you can share details of your dreams and who will listen to your frustrations. But all members of your team should be viewed as sounding boards, because they offer additional perspectives you cannot see.

One of the great benefits of a team is the ability to minimize your weaknesses. I encourage you to search for others who can do well what you do poorly. You cannot afford to be insecure or prideful if you want to be successful. You will have to entrust your team with a part of your dream without fearing they will show you up or let you down. Let me say this: even if a team member looks like the champion in the eyes

Even if a team member looks like the champion in the eyes of others, who cares if at the end of the day the check has your name on it.

of others, who cares if at the end of the day the check has your name on it.

Know that you will also be paying your team to educate you as well. Yes, you cut them a paycheck, but you also glean from their expertise and benefit from their talents. You can all learn through observation and interaction, so resist the tendency to become the be-all-to-end-all of your dream. Stay teachable and you will develop a much greater sense of what they do, how they do it, and will be able to measure their performance levels with greater accuracy.

No matter what your venture, success will follow when you build a team.

Do what you hate

Doing what you love is often followed by doing what you hate. There are many things you won't like about the dream-building process, and every dream entails doing that which you would rather not do. That's life. For example, I have met many entrepreneurs who hate dealing with the numbers, the bottom line. I explain to them that when used correctly, the numbers can tell many great stories about them and their business. The most significant thing that numbers tell is whether or not their business is actually profitable. They can determine overspending in a particular area, or make adjustments that enhance the way to best utilize financial resources.

This analogy can be applied to most things that you don't like to do. Once you learn how to conquer the dread of doing what you hate and overcome the boredom associated with it, you'll learn fascinating new skills and gain new perspectives on your dream.

My personal experience

I am a creative guy, and I was not enamored with the financial end when I first built my public relations business. I preferred to be on the cutting edge of design while leaving the numbers to someone else. However, I realized early that I needed to know all sectors of my business, and learning about numbers greatly benefitted me with my clients. Learning to analyze numbers early proved to be of great value as I moved on to other ventures.

For instance, I would often ask to look at a client's advertising budget. If a client was spending $10,000 a month on newspaper advertising, I would ask how many customers were coming in based on that $10,000. Then I would give examples of targeted ways the same money could be spent utilizing non-advertising strategies to bring in more customers. This became an "ah-ha!" moment; once they understood the numbers they could understand the strategies.

It took me years to get a grip on learning the importance of numbers. But I challenged myself to learn and understand their importance and eventually I came to enjoy the area of business finances. Today, nothing moves me until I look at the numbers.

Certainly there are people who love numbers and hate other things. The point is, you have to do what you hate in order to get to what you love. Stay focused and you will make it happen, and who knows you may begin to love doing what you once dreaded.

Take it in stride

Even with the best planning, the best advice, and wonderful teammates, you will still experience failures along the way. While failure is common to all, it takes an I'm-not-giving-up type of person to turn the setback into a learning experience. If you want to be that person, here are some things to keep in mind:

• Don't waste your time moping around and feeling sorry for yourself. You'll only lose focus and potentially give up on your plans.

• Soon after the failure, examine where the most evident problems seemed to be. You'll be able to avoid these in the future.

• Think of the events or actions that led up to the failure and design ways to avoid or minimize them.

• Be careful that you don't blame others for your mistakes, but don't take responsibility for what others may have done. If you want to achieve success, there is no room for blame shifting or ducking responsibility.

Be willing to learn as you go and grow as you learn. Stay focused on what you have in mind and continue to press forward until it comes to fruition.

You can do it!

Thoughts to Ponder

What did this chapter say to you?

What did this chapter prompt you to do?

Getting It Done Action Items

1. _____

2. _____

3. _____

4. _____

5. _____

Notes to Self

About the Author

Nolan W. McCants embodies what he has written about in this powerful little book. A self-made entrepreneur, by age 18 he owned a full-service public relations firm that ultimately represented Fortune 50 corporations, non-profit agencies, entrepreneurs, and individuals in the entertainment industry. In 1990, the U.S. Small Business Administration named him Illinois' Young Entrepreneur of the Year. Nolan was also a speaker for the Illinois Institute for Entrepreneurship Education. Nolan has authored several books, pastors a thriving ministry in south suburban Chicago, oversees an international alliance of churches, speaks internationally, and is an award winning fine arts photographer. An inspiration to thousands around the world, he continues to encourage people to pursue their dreams and live life to the fullest.

Also available from Nolan W. McCants

Wisdom to live by, lead by and grow by

Leadership Essentials

Nolan W. McCants

Foreword by Marvin E. Wiley

www.nolanmccants.com